St George's, Bloomsbury

St George's, Bloomsbury

A Hawksmoor Masterpiece Restored

Kerry Downes
Colin Amery
Gavin Stamp

Published to celebrate the completion of the restoration of this famous London church, which was generously underwritten by:

The Paul Mellon Estate
The Robert W. Wilson Challenge to Conserve Our Heritage

The Heritage Lottery Fund

English Heritage/HLF Joint Places of Worship Scheme
The Bridge House Trust
The Garfield Weston Foundation
William Shelton's Educational Foundation
The 29th May 1961 Charitable Trust
The Leche Trust
The Stuart Heath Charitable Settlement
The Historic Churches Preservation Trust
The Heritage of London Trust

Albert Gordon, Peter Stormonth Darling, Maurice Dwek, and numerous other private donors

Generous support for this publication was provided by The Paul Mellon Estate

WORLD MONUMENTS FUND

SCALA

ACKNOWLEDGEMENTS

Among those that World Monuments Fund would like to thank for their help in the restoration of St George's are the following:

Peter Aiers, Conservation Development Officer, Diocese of London; Patrick Baty, Papers and Paints; Diana Beattie, Director, Heritage of London Trust; The Rt Revd and Rt Hon Richard Chartres, Bishop of London; Canon Ronald Choppin, Building Committee; Keith Day, Sheppard Day Associates; Diocese Advisory Committee; Mike Brooks, Wallis, Special Projects Division; Rev Dr Perry Butler, Rector, St George's Bloomsbury; Gordon Cain, Cain & Co; Adrian Cave, Adrian Cave Associates; Tim Crawley and his team, Fairhaven of Anglesey Abbey; Stephen Gee, Director, Peter Inskip & Peter Jenkins Architects; John Harley, Tankerdale Conservation and Restoration; Luke Hughes, Luke Hughes & Co., Ltd; Fred Hill, Wallis, Special Projects Division; Peter Inskip, Director, Peter Inskip & Peter Jenkins Architects; Gary Jones and his team, St Blaise Conservation; Colin Kerr, Molyneux Kerr Architects; Carole Patey; Trevor Proudfoot, Cliveden Conservation; David Ball Restoration; Julian Sharpe and David and Diana Wood, Church Wardens, St George's Bloomsbury; Peter Sheppard, Sheppard Day Associates; Jane Stancliffe, Heritage Lottery Fund; Chris Watson, Gardiner & Theobald; Peter Waxman, Molyneux Kerr Architects; Rory Young, Stone carver and Conservator and members of WMF Britain's Architectural Advisory Committee: Marcus Binney, Christopher Gibbs, Donald Insall, Peter Inskip, Simon Jervis, David Lambert, Rodney Melville, Michael Morrison, Gavin Stamp and Sir Angus Stirling.

World Monuments Fund gratefully acknowledges The Brown Foundation, Inc., the Paul Mellon Estate, and Paul Beirne for their generous support of the publications program of the World Monuments Fund.

First published in 2008 by
Scala Publishers Ltd
Northburgh House
10 Northburgh Street
London EC1V 0AT, UK
www.scalapublishers.com

ISBN-13: 978-1-85759-428-7

Texts edited by Angela M. H. Schuster
Project Manager, Scala: Oliver Craske
Designer: Andrew Shoolbred
Printed and bound in China

10 9 8 7 6 5 4 3 2 1

All photographs provided by World Monuments Fund (WMF) except as follows:
Angelo Hornak/WMF: front cover, back cover, 12, 13, 15, 35, 49, 52–53 (main), 54 (both), 59–62, 66, 67, 69, 71. Richard Holttum/WMF: 2, 3, 11, 31 (lower), 33, 34, 43 (upper), 48 (bottom), 51 (all), 52 (left), 55 (middle two and lower), 56 (both), 57, 58 (upper right, lower left and lower right), 65 (all), 70. City of Westminster Archives Centre: 7, 21. All Souls College, Oxford: 14. British Library: 17 (both). RIBA Library Photographs Collection: 18, 36. Michael N. G. Frantzis/WMF: 23, 24 (top three), 25, 26 (both), 27, 43 (lower), 47 (all), 58 (upper left). © The Trustees of the British Museum: 29. Holborn Library: 30. English Heritage, National Monuments Record: 39, 40

Every effort has been made to acknowledge correct copyright of images where applicable. Any errors or omissions are unintentional and should be notified to the Publisher, who will arrange for corrections to appear in any reprints.

Page 2: Interior of St George's after restoration (west wall), August 2005.
Page 3: Original plaster cherub by Isaac Mansfield in the eastern apse, after restoration.

Contents

Foreword

The Rt Revd and Rt Hon Richard Chartres
Bishop of London

I have always loved the mobled grandeur of St George's, Bloomsbury, and it has been one of the delights of my period in office as Bishop of London to witness and make a modest contribution to the church's renaissance.

My predecessor, Edmund Gibson, "Walpole's Pope", resided at the congregation of St George's on January 28, 1730. The new church in fashionable Bloomsbury was part of the Government-supported response to rapid population growth in the capital. London, as the hub of an expanding international trading empire, was seen to need a new generation of stately churches to robe in stone those aspirations and values, beyond getting and spending, upon which any flourishing market and coherent society must depend.

Bishop Gibson's pastoral letters to the people of Middlesex also acknowledged the fragmentation of eighteenth-century society and the progress of what was then called "infidelity". St George's was built as part of a battle for the soul of London.

Of course, many people admire Hawksmoor's churches simply as architectural statements and do not subscribe to their spiritual ambition. Yet the things that perturbed Bishop Gibson are of contemporary concern.

Those involved in the polling and the work with focus groups which informed the recent general election campaigns in Britain report an almost universal lament about the erosion of common values and respect for others, together with anxiety about the collapse of moral authority, especially that of parents. Various institutions and professions were (in my view quite unfairly) blamed for this state of affairs. Politicians, the police, teachers and schools, judges – they were all frequently mentioned. The startling thing is that the Christian Church was neither blamed nor by implication regarded as having any relevant contribution to make.

The Government has made its own response to the poll findings in developing an agenda of "respect and values." Regulation and exultation alone, and what Jung called "mere appeals to ethical fraternity", are unlikely to evoke the energy needed for real transformation.

St George's in 1799, as depicted in an aquatint engraving by Thomas Malton.

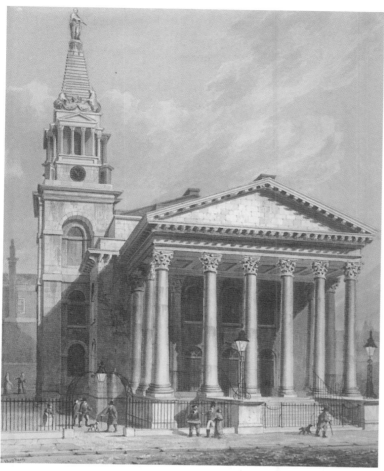

OPPOSITE A detail of
St George's as painted by
J. M. W. Turner in 1811.

LEFT Another depiction of
St George's by Thomas Malton.

The restoration of St George's as a centre for the life of its vibrant parish is part of the Church's recognition of its own responsibilities in London and in the nation in a situation where pointing the finger at others is inadequate.

But nothing could have been achieved without allies. In a way unparalleled in Europe, the Church of England is responsible for 45% of all Grade I-listed buildings in the country – an inheritance from the past which rightly belongs to the whole people of England – but lacks the level of public finance which is universal elsewhere in Europe and which (as in the case of St George's) enabled these buildings to be constructed in the first place. Everyone who loves St George's owes a huge debt of gratitude to the World Monuments Fund and its staff. The church was listed on the WMF Watch List of *100 Most Endangered Sites* in October 2002 and at the same time received a transforming bequest from the estate of the late Paul Mellon, the Anglophile American philanthropist whose love of eighteenth-century art and architecture will have a lasting memorial in this splendid restoration.

At the same time, we would still not have been able to embark upon this ambitious project but for the generous assistance of the Heritage Lottery Fund. I should like to pay tribute to the way in which the trustees and staff of the Fund have worked so hard over the past few years to ensure that a number of very significant historic church buildings realise their potential as contributors to social regeneration.

Introduction

Bonnie Burnham
President, World Monuments Fund

Corinthian columns framing the west wall, August 2005. At this stage of the restoration the interior stonework was almost complete, but construction of the new north gallery had yet to begin.

Since the World Monuments Fund launched the WMF Watch List in 1996, many extraordinary yet imperilled sacred sites have appeared on its biennial list of 100 Most Endangered Sites. In many cases, these great buildings have been largely forgotten by the public at large despite the fact that small communities are often struggling to save them, turning to the WMF for help. For many, inclusion on the Watch List represents a new beginning for a constituency that had begun to fear that its appeals would never be heard. In this context St George's, Bloomsbury is both a prime example and an exception.

The Second World War and the five decades of urban change that followed had brought the ecclesiastical works of one of Britain's finest architects, Nicholas Hawksmoor, to the verge of extinction – his six London churches having been damaged during the war, disfigured by inappropriate restorations, subjected to years of neglect, and threatened with redevelopment. Christ Church, Spitalfields, on the edge of the financial district, and St George's, Bloomsbury, near Russell Square, were both slated for demolition in a series of urban renewal schemes developed in the Sixties and Seventies. Although both were ultimately spared, thanks to the efforts of preservationists, decades of uncertainty had taken their toll on the sanctuaries, requiring a mighty effort to bring the great churches back to a worthy state.

St George's, Bloomsbury was included on WMF's 2002 Watch List, a year after it was placed on the English Heritage Register of Buildings at Risk, out of concern that its small parish, which had witnessed years of economic decline, would be unable to marshal the resources needed to renovate and maintain the huge building. Grime on the exterior and a shabby interior decor concealed the gravity of its condition, which was far more dire than it initially appeared. Following its inclusion in the Watch List, WMF in Britain, led by Colin Amery, recognised the urgency of the situation and launched a comprehensive plan to save St George's, Bloomsbury and bring together the resources necessary to do so.

Exceptionally, the project attracted support from the estate of one of the world's greatest philanthropists, the late Paul Mellon, and counterpart support from the Heritage Lottery Fund and other generous donors. Without the extraordinary investment made by The Paul Mellon Estate, which spared no expense in addressing the conservation challenges that arose, this restoration would not have been possible. Today, that effort is complete, and we can once again appreciate the church's enormous importance and enjoy its serene beauty. The results that have been achieved could scarcely have been imagined at the outset.

Atop the church's striking and original tower, huge sculptured lions and unicorns have been put back in place to call attention to an otherwise quiet classical façade. Stepping inside, one finds the awing cubic proportions of the interior, with its reconfigured nave and sedate but monumental colour scheme. The stunning reredos, restored to its original position, is a dramatic focal point.

As the colossal sculptures were raised to their positions, they heralded a new era not only for the church itself but for the entire neighbourhood surrounding it. And as St George's, Bloomsbury regains its prestige, the master designer who created it – hardly a household name even in British cultural circles – rightfully regains his place as one of the eighteenth century's greatest architects.

St George's will now become a hub of activity centring on the religious and social mission for which it was built, but with new means to sustain it as both the centre of community life and as a high expression of the commu-

The interior of St George's upon the completion of restoration in May 2008. This shows the new north gallery and the second north wall behind, viewed from the south gallery across the nave, which has been reconfigured with its original east-west orientation. The original colour scheme has been restored, and the whole interior is flooded with light once more.

The new lions and unicorns, carved by Fairhaven of Anglesey Abbey Ltd, pictured in May 2006 just after installation on the steeple of St George's.

nity's faith. Faith in the future can take many forms: it can be expressed through religious observance, but also by nurturing young people and helping them to find their path; by protecting assets, through acts of philanthropy; and by reaching beyond borders of creed, background and nationality to participate through shared values in a community beyond one's immediate circle. All of these manifestations of faith come together in historic preservation; by repairing the fabric of a building, that fabric is miraculously transformed into a vessel for new life.

For 40 years the World Monuments Fund has been engaged in this process of transformation at many sites around the world, bringing together the financial and technical resources necessary to preserve these great works and to restore their pivotal role in the local environment. WMF acts as a catalyst, initiating a process that will grow through the efforts of local partners. Every project – like the present one – provides opportunities to expand our knowledge and our know-how, to engage many individuals in this process, and to create a stronger public awareness of the important role great buildings play in all of our lives.

As we commend St George's, Bloomsbury to a more noble and confident future, we rejoice at another opportunity to demonstrate the value of our mission as defenders of the heritage of humanity. And as we complete the extraordinary accomplishment that this restoration represents, we also salute our local partners – most especially the Rector and the wardens of St George's – who have been at the centre of this effort, mobilising the consent and the enthusiasm without which this miracle could not have happened.

Hawksmoor in Perspective

Kerry Downes

awksmoor is now rightly recognised as one of the greatest of British architects, whose works speak directly to our emotions, both conscious and sometimes unconscious. For much of his life England looked towards Europe, regardless of religious differences. But political and commercial union with Scotland in 1707, the end of the long wars with France in 1713, and the 1715 Jacobite rising all contributed (among other factors) to a withdrawal from Europe and from the International Baroque. The Palladianism of Lord Burlington and Colen Campbell was promoted as specifically British, and at Hawksmoor's death (March 25, 1736) his architecture, like that of his talented colleague Sir John Vanbrugh and his master Sir Christopher Wren, was already fashionable.

Nicholas Hawksmoor was probably born early in 1662, at East Drayton, Notts., the son of a yeoman farmer. The father died, and his widow married another farmer. After a good grammar schooling the lad may have been glad to leave the step-parental home to become, a day's walk away, clerk to a Doncaster judge who came from the next village. By chance or fate, in Doncaster he met the London decorative plasterer Edward Gouge, working there. It must have struck Gouge – and maybe only then, young Nicholas – that buildings were his passion; Gouge took him to London and to Wren who gave him a job and a home.

Wren's speech was sparing but, as both office boy and surrogate elder brother to the recently widowed Wren's young children, Hawksmoor absorbed every word. He had a naïve eye for sketching buildings; now he gradually learned to draw professionally in his master's manner. He developed his idiomatic copperplate script and a flourished signature. In the office building the post-Fire City churches he learned management as well as design and construction. He noted down rates and prices. He graduated to the King's Works; before his marriage in 1696, he had left Wren's household to live in his official clerk's house at Kensington Palace. If he made all the drawings that some have attributed to him, he can hardly have slept but,

ABOVE Bust of Nicholas Hawksmoor by Henry Cheere.

OPPOSITE Keystone on the north front after restoration, June 2006.

All Souls College, Oxford. Hawksmoor designed the North Quadrangle, Hall, Buttery and Codrington Library.

while developing his own practice, he would be a right hand to Wren and later also to Vanbrugh. He was courteous, practical, businesslike, modest, and architecture was his consuming interest.

For anyone born with a gift, creativity is natural. But, like second sight or an opera singer's voice, it is also hazardous and burdensome. Natural does not equate with easy, and even obsessive industry does not guarantee flowing ideas. Metaphors for the process abound: the muse whispering in the poet's ear. Michelangelo tells of discovering – though he worked from small preliminary models – the figure hiding inside the marble block. Even in architecture he assumed the right to alter his design as building advanced and his ideas clarified; Hawksmoor then, for whom second thoughts were vital, was in extremely good company.

In the commonest metaphor, of giving birth, joy is compounded with pain and struggle – and it is relevant that the human newborn is not as fully developed as a duckling. Hawksmoor's "One can hardly avoid loving one's own children" referred to a building. Architecture is only one-third art, after gravity, convenience, coarse materials, a workforce, money. It becomes visible in the studio, public on the site. Yet parturition requires conception – private, intimate, hidden and indeed mysterious. For conception it is. I once asked a wise architect whether he started with a ground-plan. "No", he replied, "I have to start with the concept." The concept precedes clear images; it may begin as no more than a niggle in the mind. A writer told me, "The travail of writing is discovering what *exactly* it is that I want to say. When I know that, it is relatively easy."

Fifty-five years ago the complexities and quirks of Hawksmoor's architecture were seen as manifestations of someone usually out of his depth, in contrast to the (supposed) logic and clarity of the great Renaissance masters or the visceral – even shocking – bravura of Italian and Germanic Baroque. It didn't help that two of his London churches had been gutted by bombs and the others were run down; that only two were in Central London. Bloomsbury, superficially, appeared intact, yet it had never been that: within weeks of its consecration – to its architect's fury – a process of tampering had begun that never really stopped. In 1871 its most familiar feature, the steeple, lost its heraldic ornaments,[1] condemned as a weathered and tasteless joke, but now happily recreated.

It was known that the British Museum library, five minutes' walk away, held 80 original drawings for these churches. Hoping to establish that Hawksmoor was not a muddler, and aware that contemporaries did not consider him one – even the Duchess of Marlborough, who detested architects, wrote him a glowing reference – I spent part of the 1950 summer vacation studying the drawings. The rest may now be history, but there was nothing for Bloomsbury except two rejected designs. We had only the building, and the papers of the Fifty New Churches Commission which turned up in a trunk in Lambeth Palace Library. Longer and more meticulous scrutiny of the building accounts there than I could afford is the basis of the church's triumphant return to something approaching Hawksmoor's original concept. But Hawksmoor learned from Wren how to keep his designs close to his chest, and without graphic evidence of how concept became flesh, the iconologists have been obliged to speculate.

The six churches he designed for the 1711 commission are all variations on one theme, a plan generated from two axes crossing at right angles. But Bloomsbury is unique, and uniquely mysterious and moving, because its plan and disposition were also the solution to a problem none of the other interested architects had been able to solve: fitting a church with an eastern altar (required by the High Church commission) into a site already restricted by houses east and west. His concept consequently derived from an irritating problem, and it developed into a design that accepted and exploited the mismatch between the west-east axis of ritual and the south-north axis of the site.

Drawings for other churches show what trouble the steeples gave him, designs growing as the masonry rose. They show how often he changed his mind; how, through patient re-drafting – what Hawksmoor called "experience and trials, so that we are assured of the good effect" – the subtleties and refinements, of which his imagination was capable, took shape. Much has been made of his visual sources and their possible associations. Working at the peak of a tradition of wide-ranging eclecticism, his encyclopaedic historical knowledge is unsurprising: all our minds are crammed with images, visual, verbal, auditory, from whatever sphere most interests us.

But Hawksmoor's mind was not like some rambling website, to be surfed for quotations. The symphonies of Gustav Mahler, composer and conductor, are not made up of snippets from other composers' pieces. Mahler quotes himself, in a continual internal dialogue with personal resonances; music is built of what you can do with just twelve notes. Hawksmoor's quotations range widely, often arbitrarily. He did not reserve the Doric, as Serlio recommended, for heroic saints; most of Bloomsbury is Corinthian. That order is the one Vitruvius[2] says you can handle as you like,

Two elevations and a plan: early design sketches by Hawksmoor, thought to be for St George's.

17

and Hawksmoor left the pillars unfluted, the entablature mouldings unusually simple. The touching story of the Corinthian's distinctive capital deriving from an acanthus growing on a maiden's grave may evoke the after-life, but the true feminine order is the Ionic. In ancient Rome the Corinthian graces temples to Mars and Jupiter, in the Renaissance St Peter's basilica, and in London St Paul's.

The later Composite, combining Corinthian acanthus and Ionic volutes, appears inside two of the other churches and outside the Bloomsbury belfry – probably because high up at 92ft (28m) its capitals read more crisply – as well as, correctly, above the Corinthian on the north front. Yet elsewhere Hawksmoor disparaged the Composite as "a mongrel and no true species". When reason or fancy (imagination) conceived it, judgment passed it and experience ratified it, it was right to use; that was his theory and his "method architectonical". Method was not about rules: Roman architecture had few rules, and it was Renaissance architects who, assuming their existence but unable to find them, perforce invented them on the uncertain basis of surviving monuments. Although he might take a modillion cornice from the Pantheon, it was not about *copying* "Authors and Antiquity"; they preserved the "Principals," and they were like "some old father to stand by you" in the face of criticism. The spelling is deliberate: Wren distinguished *principles* (beauty,[3] strength and convenience) from *principals*, in a sense similar to that in finance meaning the capital sum that generates interest. For Wren as a Classical architect the orders were the unchanging principals, the basis of a visual syntax that expressed or implied the structural one, regardless of proportional niceties or decorative variations.

Hawksmoor liked plain surfaces and clear masses, both on the large scale of a whole building and on the smaller scale of details like the giant triple keystones of the basement windows at Bloomsbury. This particular motif occurs elsewhere in his churches; it originates in sixteenth-century European Mannerism, but as usual Hawksmoor transcends his source: bigger, bolder, more emphatic. They imply both strength and, rhetorically, the possibility of weakness, since one keystone smoothly embedded in the masonry is all the structure needs. He uses finer details – in the mouldings of the interior Corinthian order, the ceilings, and the keystones of the broad half-oval internal arches – to define for the eye the parts that make up the whole, like the rhymes and punctuations in a sonnet.

But the heart of St George's is its interior ambiguity: not now the chaos of generations of tinkering but a considered and deliberate ambiguity restored by the reconstructed north gallery and the re-oriented altar. Entering under the portico you face a side gallery but also a sequence of theatrical arches. Entering under the tower you face the altar, a gallery on either side. Whichever way you enter, what you see is unexpected, disorienting, but calculated. The bright clerestory above (the "cupola" in the building commission's minutes, the "lantern" in the billbooks) is square in plan, but its ceiling divisions read two ways. Something analogous but different occurs in all the churches; this is the "strangeness in the proportion" that the great Jacobean rationalist Francis Bacon found in all beauty. Hawksmoor's geom-

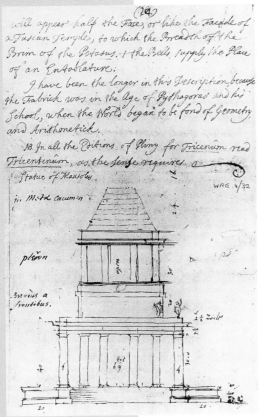

Hawksmoor's sketch inspired by the tomb of Mausolus at Halicarnassus (Bodrum, in Turkey), one of the Seven Wonders of the Ancient World.

etry is plain and bold but not simple: it speaks to the soul, inspiring awe. The notion of the subconscious is not the invention of psychoanalysis: in Hawksmoor's day it was called "memory" and much studied. Hawksmoor is a *great* architect because of his powerful and intuitive understanding of the capacity of abstract forms to move the human spirit.

Strangeness is also at the heart of the steeple. Wren's circle was not the first to spend Sunday afternoon reconstructing such lost ancient wonders as the tomb of Mausolus at Halicarnassus (some of whose sculptures are now in the British Museum), a huge structure culminating in a stepped pyramid. Hawksmoor's pyramid has more to do with shape than with archaeology, much more to do with a child's box of bricks. It was, and remains, different from all other steeples. And, as in a dream, it becomes a hatchment as the heraldic lion and unicorn (England and Scotland) fight for the crown. Mausolus never appeared atop his pyramid, but it was not inappropriate to place the head of the Anglican church on a steeple – such a commemoration was long contemplated. The commission was less disconcerted by the animals than by Hawksmoor's failure to ask approval for them, "though some sort of decorations were necessary in these places". And no commissioner ever forgot the image – and neither, reader, will you!

1. Although G. E. Street enjoyed them.
2. Vitruvius's *De Architectura* is the only surviving Roman treatise on architecture.
3. Vitruvius's word is *venustas*, which means attractiveness.

ABOVE LEFT Hawksmoor's early design for a tower for St George's.

ABOVE The statue of King George I standing atop the steeple of St George's, photographed before restoration. The original lions and unicorns which had been mounted at the bottom of the steeple had been replaced in 1871 by stone carvings of "knots of cloth".

I will not cease from mental fight
Nor shall the sword sleep in my hand
Till we have built Jerusalem
In England's green and pleasant land.

WILLIAM BLAKE (1757–1827)

Building a New Jerusalem:
The Fifty New Churches Act of 1711

Colin Amery

A quest to build Jerusalem in England's green and pleasant land began nearly a century before William Blake composed his poem, precipitated by the collapse of the roof of the church of St Alfege in Greenwich, on the night of November 28, 1710. Following the collapse, church parishioners sent a petition to the House of Commons, asking Parliament to grant £6000 for St Alfege to be rebuilt. The parishioners had for 40 years contributed to the building of St Paul's Cathedral and other churches through a tax on coal and they felt that, as the cathedral was almost finished, the coal taxes should be made available to repair and build other London churches.

As St Alfege collapsed, so did the long-running government of the Whig party, which fell after 22 years of power. The new Tory House of Commons seized the opportunity to review the whole question of church building in the capital. Since the Great Fire of London in 1666, the city's built-up area had vastly increased. Wren had rebuilt a plenitude of churches in the fire-wrecked centre of the city itself, but the new suburbs were growing around old village settlements like Shoreditch, Holborn, Whitechapel, Stepney, and Southwark, and had large populations that had outgrown the small medieval churches that survived. Thousands of people were unable to go to a church and the once rural parishes could not fulfil the role expected of them to maintain law and order and the welfare of their parishioners.

The Tory landslide in the election of 1710 was a victory for the High Church party, and so in 1711, with the enthusiastic support of Queen Anne herself, an Act of Parliament was passed imposing a duty on coal for the specific purpose "of building fifty new churches of stone and other proper materials, with towers or steeples to each of them; and for purchasing of sites of churches and church yards, and burying places, in or near the cities of London and Westminster, or the suburbs thereof; and for making such chapels as are already built, and capable thereof, Parish Churches and for purchasing houses for the habitations of the Ministers of the said churches..." [1]

Commissioners were appointed under the leadership of the Archbishop of Canterbury, and among a large group of Tory prelates were three architects – Sir Christopher Wren, Sir John Vanbrugh and Thomas Archer. The surveyors the Commissioners selected to carry out this great church-building programme were Nicholas Hawksmoor and William Dickinson. Both of them had worked with Wren as draughtsmen in connection with the city churches and Dickinson was Wren's Deputy Surveyor to the fabric of Westminster Abbey. Wren wrote to the surveyors in a practical way drawing on the 40 years of his own church-building experience, advocating a modest approach, proposing churches similar to his relatively plain and simple church of St James's on Piccadilly. Vanbrugh, on the other hand, advocated enthusiastically that the new churches should be monuments to the posterity and piety of the Queen and ornaments to the city and the nation.

In many ways the 50 new churches were to be monuments to the Tory victory and stressed a return to the liturgical practices of the early Church. One of the Commissioners – Sir Peter King, in fact a Whig – had written *An Enquiry into the Constitution, Discipline, Unity, and Worship of the Primitive Church*, and in the records of the Commission is a plan by Nicholas Hawksmoor of a "Basilica after the Primitive Christians," which underscored the way the Commissioners were thinking both architecturally and ritualistically. The Commissioners envisaged large and expensive buildings with handsome porticoes and towers, which, in addition to serving London's growing population, would offer an opportunity to secure an Anglican presence amid increasing numbers of Catholics and Dissenters.

Construction of the churches had barely begun, however, when the Tory government fell in July 1714. The same year, the pious Queen Anne died and was succeeded by the Hanoverian King George I. The generous vision of the original Commission was changed by a new Commission set up in 1715, which decided not to build 50 churches but to complete merely those that had already been started, as the funds were running out. In the end, only twelve churches were finished, six of which were designed by Hawksmoor: St Alfege, Greenwich; St Anne's, Limehouse; St George's-in-the-East; St Mary's, Woolnoth; Christ Church, Spitalfields; and St George's, Bloomsbury.

Hawksmoor remained a Commissioner from 1711 until his death in 1736. His churches are undoubtedly the grandest built in England between the Reformation and the nineteenth century and they are a demonstration that, even in an officially Protestant country, the Baroque style can have a power and force to inspire awe and respect – as much for the ceremonial of the Anglican Establishment as for any observance or commemoration of the Divine presence. The rhetoric of the Baroque language in Hawksmoor's hands is both grand and disturbing in these churches. They are all different and original – heavy with archaeological sources and profound in their architectural abstraction. Money from the coal mines paid for the stones – deep sources from the earth to create flagship temples for the State religion.

Elevation drawing of the finished church.

1. *Statutes of the Realm* ix, p 473 (9 Anne, Cap xvii); *Statutes at Large* iv, pp 487–89 (9 Anne, Cap xxii). In 1721 the various statutes were published separately under the title *The Acts of Parliament relating to the Building of Fifty New Churches in and about The Cities of London and Westminster*.

Hawksmoor and his Six London Churches

Colin Amery

Nicholas Hawksmoor had a dream. Not a dream of the mystic variety described in Peter Ackroyd's disturbing popular novel, *Hawksmoor*, but a dream of rivalry in Europe; of a race for splendour in the cities of Paris, Rome and London. He dreamed of great buildings in England that would challenge the magnificence of urban design under Louis XIV and Jean-Baptiste Colbert in France and the dazzling architectural achievements in Rome under Pope Sixtus V. And in his six London churches, Hawksmoor began to make this dream a reality.

It is not difficult to imagine Hawksmoor in his London house wanting to see his own city as some kind of new Rome. Although he never went abroad, we know from the catalogue of the sale of his library that he was an avid collector of prints, folios and books, especially of Roman antiquities and reconstructions of works of the antique. If we see him as the English equivalent of Francesco Borromini (1599–1667) – both of them independent, imaginative, complex and dynamic – we can see how fortunate it was that the Fifty New Churches Act coincided with the high point of Hawksmoor's creativity. London suddenly could become a new and original classical city able to hold its own with any European rival. Hawksmoor's knowledge and talent were ready.

For much of Hawksmoor's early life, England had looked towards Europe for its architectural and artistic inspiration. The final victory over France and the Peace of Utrecht in 1713 brought to an end a series of expensive continental wars and created, in the last years of Queen Anne's reign, a sense of national Protestant pride. It was her Tory government that promoted the Fifty New Churches Act to enshrine the Anglican triumph. When George I succeeded Anne in 1714 and the Whig party defeated the Tories, architecture was used in a way to assert British independence and express relief that the nation was free of continental and Catholic influences. This second decade of the eighteenth century in England was to see great architectural opportunities after the wars but also confusion in the debate over the most appropriate public architectural style.

Christ Church, Spitalfields, one of the six London churches designed by Hawksmoor.

Three views of St Alfege,
Greenwich.

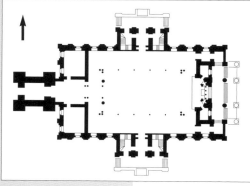

Plan of St Alfege, Greenwich.

In 1715 Colen Campbell (1673–1729) published *Vitruvius Britannicus*,
which became the defining work for all English Palladian architects, led by
Lord Burlington (1694–1753) who built and preached according to absolute
classical standards and rules. Palladianism, based upon the works of Andrea
Palladio (1508–1580), was seen as a purer style, in opposition to the more
imaginative, slightly wild and dramatic English Baroque style perfected by
Vanbrugh and Hawksmoor. Sobriety appeared to be favoured over drama,
Protestantism over Counter-Reformation Catholicism. As the style of Palladianism triumphed in England, it made Hawksmoor's architecture look
extravagantly original.

Of course, architectural history is never a simple battle of the styles.
What is clear is that at the beginning of the eighteenth century Hawksmoor
interpreted the sources of antiquity with imagination and personal genius
while the Palladians followed those surveyors of the antique world, Sebas-
tiano Serlio (1475–1554) and Andrea Palladio, in a quest for formal classical
perfection. Nowhere is Hawksmoor's adventurous quest more dramatically

St George's-in-the-East, Wapping.

played out than it is across the whole range of his six London churches. With their massive bulk, soaring height, and dramatic use of light and shade, they provide a distinctive punctuation to the architectural landscape on both sides of the Thames.

St Alfege (1712–1714) in Greenwich was the first of the churches to be built under the 1711 Act of Parliament. As shown in the plan, there is a central space and two axes, the longer running from east to west with the cross axis marked, in this case, by two transepts: all features characteristic of Hawksmoor's other churches, as too were the flat ceiling and the richly decorated auxiliary spaces. The tower was finished by John James in 1730 and is insignificant compared to the rest of the mighty composition. The exterior is smooth with round-headed windows that contrast with the heavy, keystoned square ones. The portico at the east end is plain yet majestic, with its Doric columns and Roman arch that breaks through the pediment. The interior was gutted by bombing during the Second World War, but restored by 1953, when it was rededicated.

Christ Church, Spitalfields (1714–1729) suffered in the late nineteenth century from alterations made by the Victorian architect Ewan Christian, and during the last few decades from neglect and the threat of inappropriate reuse schemes. A recent restoration has returned the church back to its sumptuous, pre-1850 classical interior. A central space with a flat ceiling is flanked by aisles roofed with elliptical barrel vaults, carried on a raised composite order. These classical elements give the Hawksmoor interior a deeply Roman character. The exterior is punctuated with plain, bold and massive elements, including round clerestory windows positioned by Hawksmoor to create a dramatic play of light and shade. A Tuscan porch with a semicircular pediment is attached to the west end, and with the tower and spire immediately behind it, the whole composition is quite overwhelming for any viewer. At the east end, there is a Venetian window. This may indicate the growing popularity of the Palladians, or it might simply be echoing the arched pediment of the entrance portico.

St George's-in-the-East (also 1714–1729) in Wapping, East London, is now a roofless shell with a small new church built within its original walls. As at St Anne's, Limehouse, and Christ Church, Spitalfields, it has two right-angled axes. The cross axis is marked with stair towers set towards the cor-

BELOW St Anne's, Limehouse.

BELOW RIGHT St Mary, Woolnoth.

ners rather than the transepts, as at St Alfege. The whole external composition with its two towers, the horizontal box of the nave, and the wide principal tower, creates one of the finest English Baroque compositions.

St Anne's, Limehouse, built from 1714 to 1730, is not as elemental in its external composition as St George's-in-the-East. It was gutted by fire in 1850, but painstakingly restored from 1851 to 1854 by John Morris. It is based on a four-column plan with east and west transepts. But like St George's-in-the-East, the tower is Gothic in spirit. As at all of the six churches, the ceiling is flat and the emphasis is on the cross axis.

St Mary, Woolnoth, in the city of London, was built from 1716 to 1727, and is unlike any of the other five Hawksmoor churches. It differs both in plan, being based on a square, and in its elements, with the external rustication and decorated blind niches of the south side being more Mannerist than Baroque or Antique. Unlike Hawksmoor's other churches, the tower at St Mary's is very broad, occupying almost the full width of the west front.

Built between 1716 and 1731, St George's, Bloomsbury has been hailed as Hawksmoor's greatest London church, its impressive Corinthian portico on the south elevation vividly recalling the grandeur of Imperial Rome. This was the first time this feature had been used in a London church, and at none of the other five churches does he use the Corinthian order. The tower also differentiates St George's from the other five. It is centrally placed on the west side and is square rather than rectangular, continuing right down to the ground. It is often considered to be the most whimsical of all Hawksmoor's church towers, with its stepped spire, statue of George I, and its blatant reference to the Mausoleum of Halicarnassus. Two crowned unicorns and two crowned lions that originally graced the sides of the spire were removed in 1871. The north elevation is punctuated with a two-storey arcade, positioned over the massive keystones of the crypt windows.

Collectively, the six London churches form the bulk of Hawksmoor's oeuvre – along with the West Towers of Westminster Abbey – and demonstrate the qualities that make him the most significant of English Baroque architects, making their neglect even harder to fathom.

Hawksmoor's West Towers of Westminster Abbey.

The Setting

Colin Amery

Hogarth's 1751 engraving
Gin Lane, part of a campaign
against the alcoholic spirit
which had become the plague
of London. The dissolute,
emaciated population depicted
by Hogarth can be seen falling
victim in a variety of ways
to the evils of gin. In the
background is the tower
of St George's church.

The church is always known as 'St George's, Bloomsbury', partly to distinguish it from all other London churches of that name – it is one of ten churches dedicated to Britain's patron saint, including a neighbouring one in Queen's Square. Bloomsbury also has a certain ring to it, evoking the literary and artistic Bloomsbury of the early twentieth century, the Bloomsbury of the Group – Lady Ottoline Morrell around the corner from the church in her drawing room in Gower Street, and Virginia Woolf and her coterie at home in Fitzroy Square. A loose association of friends, mostly writers and artists, the Bloomsbury Group subscribed to the philosophy of George Moore, believing that "by far the most valuable things... are... the pleasures of human intercourse and the enjoyment of beautiful objects... It is they... that form the rational ultimate end of social progress." While it is doubtful that any of these literary figures ever did more than pass by St George's, the philosophy they espoused provided inspiration for WMF in Britain as it organised the recent restoration of the church, underwritten by its friends and supporters, mostly from America.

Today, Hawksmoor's late masterpiece is again a "beautiful object," despite the fact that Bloomsbury is a far cry from the elegant enclave of Georgian architecture it once was, with streets of perfectly proportioned stock brick houses and smoking chimneys from winter coal fires. Yet, with a little imagination, one can visualise the giant, white Portland stone hulk of St George's rising above the austere elevations and the smoke-filled atmosphere of an expanding Georgian city when the church was built. At that time, the architectural taste of the English had not moved far from that described a century earlier by Inigo Jones, the father of English classicism with its undemonstrative and uniform elevations. But never underestimate the Englishman, as Jones noted; while he inwardly may prefer "a gravity in publick places", behind the orderly façade "he hath his immaginacy set on fire, and sumtimes licenciously flying out." But this gaunt giant looming over nascent Bloomsbury, as seen in William Hogarth's famed 1751 engraving *Gin Lane*,

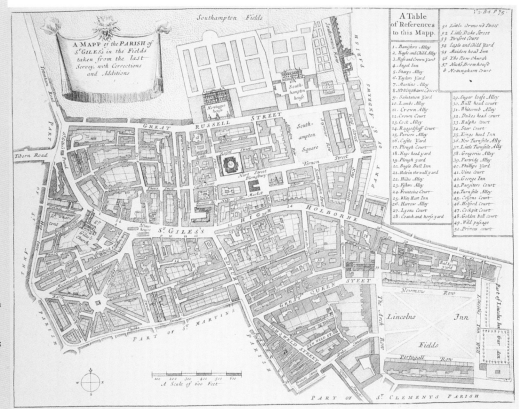

must have seemed extraordinary to mid-eighteenth-century Londoners, including Hogarth. In his lively way he rather plays up the absurdity of King George I on top of the steeple looking down on sodden working-class Londoners. It was only a few years after the publication of this engraving (along with another entitled *Beer Street*) that Hogarth's *Analysis of Beauty* appeared, which put the study of the ancient world at the centre of artistic inspiration. Hogarth must also have seen this quality in Hawksmoor's church, and in his engraving its strange tower hovers as a metaphor for the triumph of enlightened order over chaos in London's streets.

The history of St George's in many ways parallels that of Bloomsbury itself, an area that is today bounded by Tottenham Court Road to the west, Gray's Inn Road to the east, Euston Road to the north, and New Oxford Street and Bloomsbury Way to the south. Until New Oxford Street was cut through in 1847 the church, which lies on the southern boundary of Bloomsbury, was in close to notorious slums. But it had not always been that way.

During the early seventeenth century, informal groups of houses had begun to be built in Bloomsbury. In 1661 the Earl of Southampton began to impose a formal plan on his estate with his building of Bloomsbury Square and a few streets to the west and south. His own abode, Southampton House – later Bedford House – was a long, low, brick residence that occupied the north side of Bloomsbury Square until it was demolished in 1800. Through a second marriage, the Countess of Southampton acquired stepchildren; one of her stepdaughters later married Lord John Russell, who became the Duke of Bedford upon his father's death, inheriting most of Bloomsbury.

Two other mansions – Montagu House, completed 1679 (later the first home of the British Museum) and Thanet House, completed 1686 – were built on land leased from the Russell family, creating a street of grand houses, Great Russell Street, which now passes in front of the British Museum. At that time it was on the northern edge of the metropolis and enjoyed views to the distant hills of Highgate and Hampstead.

Residents of this up-and-coming genteel and elegant area were part of the parish of St Giles-in-the-Fields, and to attend that church they had to pass through the area known as the Rookery – portrayed so graphically in Hogarth's *Gin Lane* – at the risk of life and limb. The residents petitioned for a new church in their neighbourhood and were successful under the legislation for the Fifty New Churches Act in 1711. The only land available, however, was a tight site on Hart Street – now Bloomsbury Way – surrounded by houses owned by the widow of Lord John Russell, Duke of Bedford. It was purchased for £1,000.

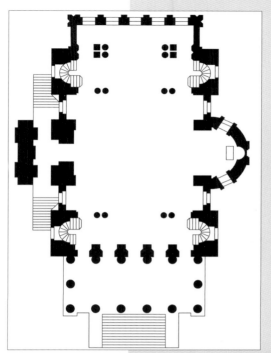

The Design

Colin Amery

The six churches Hawksmoor designed for the 1711 commission are all variations on one theme, a plan generated from two axes crossing at right angles. But Bloomsbury is unique, and uniquely mysterious and moving, because its plan and disposition were also the solution to the problem none of the other interested architects had been able to solve: fitting a church with an eastern altar (required by the High Church commission) into a site already restricted by houses east and west.

As it is at St George's, Hawksmoor had to exercise his sense of grandeur and tradition within a site that, being closely embraced by domestic architecture, has never been big enough for the church. Today, one must stand away from the church on the opposite side of Bloomsbury Way to understand the scale of the portico, trying to imagine that the red brick flats to the left and the hotel to the right are modest four-storey Georgian houses. So what then is it that Hawksmoor wanted us to see? First of all, it is perhaps the most grandiose of London's eighteenth-century church fronts – grander than St Martin-in-the-Fields and stronger and more elevated than St George's, Hanover Square. It is also very Roman. Its portico is as close as one can get to a reconstruction in eighteenth-century London of the Temple of Bacchus (perhaps appropriate for *Gin Lane*) at Baalbek. Although Hawksmoor never saw that building firsthand, he knew it well, having provided some drawings of it for a book, *A Journey from Aleppo to Jerusalem at Easter AD 1697*, by Henry Maundrell (1665–1701), an Oxford-educated clergyman who had been chaplain to English merchants in Aleppo, Syria. Hawksmoor drew upon another book, *Architecture Française* by Jean Marot, for information on what the temple looked like; its actual measurements came from another British chaplain with archaeological interests who was serving in Syria. Hawksmoor wasn't just interested in the archaeology; he looked at great buildings like Baalbek as sources for his own design process. The Temple of Bacchus was twice the size, at least, of St George's and on a large open site, and its columns were monolithic. Perhaps Hawksmoor also had in mind a

Interior of the church during restoration; the lower areas of the wall have yet to be painted.

The portico and tower of St George's from the southeast, viewed from Bloomsbury Way before restoration. To left and right are the adjoining buildings. St George's has always existed on a cramped site.

more urban ancient precedent, the Pantheon in Rome, with its spectacularly deep portico. Hawksmoor's portico has six columns (hexastyle) while the Pantheon has eight (octastyle), with fluted columns, but it has the same deep projection. If one looks carefully one can see Hawksmoor has two pediments – one on the front of the portico, and a subsidiary one that supports the roof of the central clerestory, the latter with a demi-lune window at its centre. While it is barely discernable from street level, it is a masterly piece of cohesive design and it is the first external clue of Hawksmoor's planning device that he uses so often for his churches – that of a square within a square.

At St George's, the inner square is pushed up higher than the outer to make a clerestory to light the nave. The overall impression that the portico gives – elevated at the top of a great flight of granite steps – is of the Corinthian order expressing Roman seriousness and presence in the city. Of course, the problem with St George's is that one would expect this grand entry to lead the eye to the altar, indeed one expects to be on the axis of the altar. But the nature of the site meant that the axis directly in front of the viewer as he enters is to the north and not the liturgical east. We'll return to that dilemma when we discuss the interior. But it is relevant to the location of the tower which, as well as supporting its extraordinary spire, marks the west entrance to the church with two flights of steps that lead up to the doors – one from the north and one from the south. Yet, however strong and strange the architecture of the tower, it is the portico that lures the visitor into the church: it says so clearly, *This is the entrance.*

Hawksmoor scholar Kerry Downes has described the tower so well – as he says, one needs to look at it as a giant royal hatchment, a pyramid that has more to do with shape than with archaeology, much more to do with a child's box of bricks. On top of this, standing on a Roman altar in Roman dress, is that well-known imperial figure, King George I of Hanover. When the church was completed, it had the lions and the unicorns on the corners of the stepped steeple, fighting for the crown. These life-size creatures were removed in 1871 as "very doubtful ornaments," the whole tower having earlier been described by Horace Walpole as "a masterpiece of absurdity." That great architect Charles Robert Cockerell (1788–1863) remarked on seeing the tower in the background of Hogarth's *Gin Lane* that "Hawksmoor was scarcely sober when he designed it." There is also the well-known anonymous rhyme –

> When Harry the Eighth left the pope in the lurch
> His Parliament made him the head of the church.
> But George's good subjects, the Bloomsbury people,
> Instead of the church, made him head of the steeple.

If one walks to the rear of the church on Little Russell Street, one is presented with one of the best architectural surprises in London. The north side of the church is a different building and in this quiet street is Hawksmoor's brilliant elevation, massive and dignified, a huge pediment over five bays with two storeys and two different classical orders. The arched windows give it the air of a secular palace that has strayed to London from Rome. The ground level of the façade is hugely over-scaled and the pediment is delicate so that the perspective is strangely enhanced. The most marvellous things in this view are the massive, elemental keystones on the ground level that, quite deliberately, give a sense of a giant temple that is still to be completely excavated. Hawksmoor wants us to feel curious about this immense Roman edifice – almost as though it was all there before and he has just rediscovered it. Each of the four elevations of the church is different and it is only when one goes inside that the great height and the enormous ceiling begin to unify the complexity of the architecture.

What Hawksmoor excelled at in his churches and in his great interiors at Blenheim and Easton Neston was his understanding of the dramatic possibilities of light and shade and an ability to play with architectural elements in a dynamic way.

The great interior of St George's is far more solemn and initially appears more empty than the vaulted and coffered interior of Christ Church, Spitalfields. If one stands with one's back to the east apse, one faces a huge western wall apparently almost devoid of detail. But look carefully and one senses the whole composition is a giant Venetian arch. Hawksmoor wants us to sense the huge thickness of the walls and the weight of the tower – we may be in a Georgian church but we are also in a temple. We ought not to forget that this is an interior of high seriousness. This new creation drawn from the Old World – Halicarnassus and Baalbek brought to London – would have been spectacularly reinforced by the quality of the light pouring in from clear glass windows, many of which were later replaced by indifferent Victorian stained glass.

In all of Hawksmoor's London churches there is a "strangeness in the proportion" that the great Jacobean rationalist Francis Bacon found in all beauty. Hawksmoor's sense of proportion was probably reinforced by the galleries he was persuaded to add; helping to create a "double-cube" effect. His geometry is plain and bold but not simple: it speaks to the soul, inspiring awe. The notion of the subconscious is not the invention of psychoanalysis: in Hawksmoor's day it was called "memory" and was much studied. Hawksmoor is a great architect because of his powerful and intuitive understanding of the capacity of abstract forms to move the human spirit.

The steeple and pediment after restoration, with the new lions and unicorns in place, viewed from the southeast in June 2006.

The Church through Time

Gavin Stamp

St George's, Bloomsbury is at once the grandest and the most eccentric of Nicholas Hawksmoor's London churches. Furthermore, because of its awkward site, it was the one with the most unusual and ingenious plan. The site in Bloomsbury purchased in 1716 did not allow a freestanding monument, like the churches in Spitalfields, Wapping and Limehouse. The ground was (and is) confined by existing buildings to both east and west, and was much wider from north to south. Several architects grappled with the difficulties of fitting a church onto this site before Hawksmoor's second scheme was adopted. The essential problem was that a conventional east-west orientated rectangular building, or even a square one, would not fit. A church here could, of course, have been orientated north-south, but the traditional Christian orientation towards the east seems to have been important for Hawksmoor as for the 1711 Commissioners. He therefore came up with a solution that seemed symmetrical internally but which was, in fact, asymmetrical about the east-west axis, for there was but one aisle to the south and two to the north of the centralised, cross-axial space that formed the nave, or the body of the church.

To the south of the south aisle was placed the grand hexastyle Corinthian portico (and if it was objected that this did not lead directly to the altar, as in a temple, but lay at one side of the church, Hawksmoor surely was well aware that the traditional entrance to an English church always lay on the south side). To the west was placed a semi-detached tower, which also served as an entrance, with staircases on either side allowing access from both north and south. This tower defined the position of the liturgical axis, whose eastern end was stressed by the protruding apse in which Hawksmoor placed the communion table to the east. As in all of his churches, the centrality of the congregational area was emphasised by a symmetrical cross-axis, running north-south, and here the symmetry of a perfectly square space – rising to a cube – was defined by the clerestory above and, at a lower level, by walls to east and west and by galleries between the internal supporting columns to north and south. The asymmetry created by

Sketch of St George's by the surveyor William Newton, 1762.

RIGHT View of St George's in the mid-twentieth century, with the roof of the British Museum Reading Room and Senate House visible in the distance.

BELOW The funeral of the suffragette Emily Davison was held at St George's on June 14, 1913. Davison had run onto Epsom racecourse during the running of the Derby and been trampled by the king's horse, dying of her injuries; it is not clear whether her intentions were suicidal or whether it was an accidental collision that occurred during a protest. Her funeral cortege attracted large crowds and was a major event in the campaign for women's suffrage.

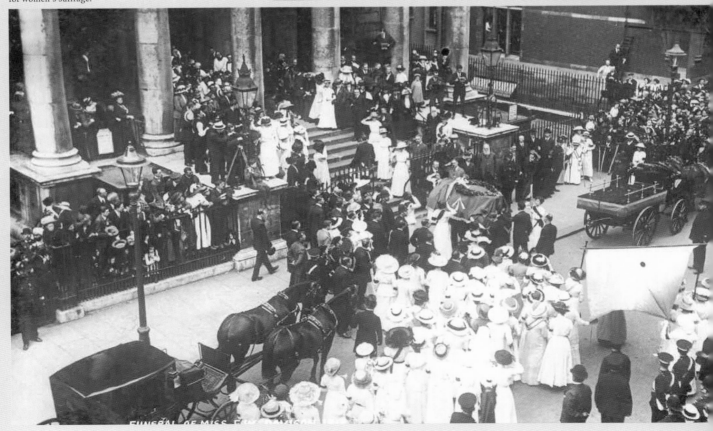

FUNERAL OF MISS EMILY DAVISON

the additional north aisle (to serve as a vestry and parish room) was, there-fore, not immediately appreciated. This was all very clever but St George's was – until the recent restoration – the most difficult to comprehend of all Hawksmoor's churches as it was the most radically altered internally, so that it required a considerable effort to imagine the interior as its designer intended it to be.

St George's was not the only Hawksmoor church to be altered. Indeed, it is remarkable that during the half-century after the Second World War, which saw the revival of the architect's reputation and increasing reverence for his work, there was not a single church with its original interior intact and unal-tered to testify without ambiguity to the architect's original intentions. Several, of course, had been gutted by the enemy bombs that, fortunately, missed his Bloomsbury masterpiece. Of these, St John's, Horselydown was subsequently

During the Second World War the church was photographed as part of the National Buildings Record, a project set up in 1941 to docu-ment for posterity important monuments as a record against possible bomb damage. This view shows the reredos in the north of the nave; the ground level windows had been walled up since the 1870s.

demolished; St George's-in-the-East survived but was not restored (a clever new church, by Arthur Bailey, being built within the walls); and St Alfege, Greenwich was reconstructed internally by Sir Albert Richardson closely following its pre-war arrangement. St Anne's, Limehouse had also been gutted by fire, but a century earlier, and had been rebuilt after 1850 by Philip Hardwick. St Mary, Woolnoth had lost its galleries during the reordering carried out by William Butterfield in 1875–76. And Christ Church, Spitalfields had also lost its galleries and had been much altered in the internal reconstruction perpetrated by Ewan Christian in 1866, all happily reinstated in the recently completed restoration. But it was St George's, Bloomsbury which had been most changed, and rendered most incomprehensible, particularly by the radical reorientation of 1781, carried out by Thomas Rogers.

St George's has, in fact, suffered from a series of alterations and changes right through its history. As so often in the history of architecture, an ingenious solution to a particular problem was not generally understood and so rapidly altered. A west gallery was installed almost immediately after consecration – without reference either to the Commissioners or their architect – and then, after some years of deliberation, the whole interior was reorientated under the direction of the surveyor, Thomas Rogers. The reredos was moved from its apse to the north wall of the extra aisle and a north-south liturgical axis established by removing the central portion of the north gallery. It must be admitted that this solution was as logical as it was ingenious, for the depressed elliptical arches that rose above the colonnades dividing nave from aisles and north aisle from vestry then read as a series of transverse arches, framing the view from the doors in the south portico and leading the eye towards the reredos – with the north aisles, indeed, now forming a discrete chancel. The reredos, communion table, pulpit, and other expensive furnishings were also altered as they were moved about the church following reorientation and subsequent reorderings. Fortunately, discarded timberwork was often re-used, but among the most serious losses is that of the pulpit's sounding board. Moving the reredos and communion table to the north had also resulted in windows in the north wall being successively walled up, while other windows were filled with stained glass instead of the original clear Crown glass. A peripatetic organ was first installed in 1788 in a new east gallery (blocking the original apsidal chancel) and eventually ended up in the south gallery in the 1950s.

The most coherent alterations to the interior after those of 1781 were carried out in 1871–72 by the distinguished church architect George Edmund Street, designer of the Royal Courts of Justice. Like so many Georgian churches, St George's was altered to conform with changed notions of dignified worship. The reredos was raised and a larger chancel, with choir stalls, created in the old north aisles, while some galleries were removed and the closed box pews – so abhorrent to the Victorians – were cut down and lost their doors. More stained glass windows were inserted and a tiled floor was laid down. It might be expected that Street, as a committed Gothicist, would have had little respect for the Classical architecture of St George's, but in fact little of Hawksmoor's original interior fabric was actually lost. The most regrettable alteration carried out was external: the removal of the stone

TOP The reredos situated on the north wall, photographed before restoration.

ABOVE The south of the church before restoration; in the gallery was the organ, which had been moved there in the 1950s.

OPPOSITE The south gallery in the 1940s, photographed as part of the National Buildings Record project.

lions and unicorns carved by Edward Strong the Elder that gambolled at the corners of the base of the stepped Tomb of Mausolus steeple. Hawksmoor had originally been reprimanded for ordering these heraldic beasts without permission from the Commissioners, and they had often been lampooned. Street's excuse for replacing them with knots of cloth to terminate the original carved garlands was that they were very decayed, but that serious High Churchman probably regarded them as unacceptably frivolous.

Further alterations to the woodwork of the interior and to the organ were carried out in the 1880s and 1890s by Charles Fitzroy Doll, surveyor to the Bedford Estate and architect of the Hotel Russell. A little earlier, at the end of the 1870s, a vestry house had been built at the north-west corner of the site, designed by Joseph Peacock.

The contribution of the twentieth century to St George's was chiefly to try to undo the alterations of the nineteenth. Work was carried out in the 1930s by Sir Charles Nicholson and in the 1970s by Laurence King, whose contribution was essentially trivial where it was not destructive and largely consisted of commissioning the decorators Campbell Smith to apply blue paint and gilding where none had been before. Extraordinarily, having escaped damage during the Second World War, St George's was briefly threatened with demolition in 1962 by the abortive project to build a new British Library south of the British Museum. However, the architects of the library, Sir Leslie Martin and Colin St John Wilson, insisted on preserving the church as a freestanding monument. Shorn of its context and with the asymmetrical east and west elevations cruelly exposed, Hawksmoor's unusual plan would have been rendered all the more incomprehensible if the redevelopment plan had gone through.

Although it survived, St George's was neglected and its physical condition deteriorated. After serving as the University of London's church in the 1960s, pastoral difficulties and the depopulation of its parish left its small congregation struggling. In 2000, following the collapse of part of the portico ceiling, English Heritage decided to place this Grade I-listed church on their Buildings at Risk Register and soon afterwards it was proposed as a candidate for the World Monuments Fund's Watch List. The WMF in Britain highlighted its neglect in a campaign which was to win the support of the Paul Mellon estate, anxious to help restore an eighteenth-century building that Mr Mellon, a great connoisseur of British art and architecture of that period, would have appreciated.

A full and expensive restoration could not have been contemplated without international support, and this, in turn, encouraged the Heritage Lottery Fund to contribute handsomely. In contrast to the restoration of Christ Church, Spitalfields, which took over 30 years, that of St George's was to follow a rapid and sophisticated programme, and was completed in the spring of 2008, six years after it began.

ABOVE Gilded and painted capitals before restoration.

OPPOSITE AND BELOW The north-south orientated nave before restoration, showing the blue ceiling and extensive gilding introduced in the early 1970s.

The first arrangement of Hawksmoor's interior included 68 box pews on the main level, each with four seats, with further seating in two galleries: twelve pews in the south gallery and sixteen pews in the north. The galleries defined a symmetrical space for the nave, with the north gallery and its screen separating the nave from the vestry and parish room in the far north bay. By the time the church was completed, the site was hemmed in by new houses to the east and west. Any additional seating had to be fitted within the existing structure.

1719–26	1776	1880s
1731	1817	up to 2003
1762	1870s	2006–08

PRINCIPAL LEVEL GALLERIES

Hawksmoor, 1719–26

Hawksmoor's original arrangement of the church, in the form of a classical temple oriented externally north to south, fitting the layout of the plot. The insertion of the north gallery separated the northernmost bay of the interior, thereby creating a separate parish room, and formed a symmetrical, east-facing nave. Part of Hawksmoor's original planning of the principal level of the church was the arrangement of the box pews in a collegiate format, aligned on the sanctuary, which also gave it a unity with the gallery.

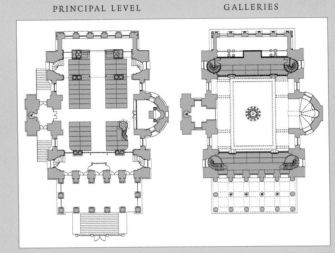

Wither, 1731

Mr Wither, a local builder, was commissioned by the Select Vestry to build a west gallery with funds lent by a Mr Milner, a member of the parish. Hawksmoor, incensed with the alteration of his design, wrote to the Church Commissioners:

> "upon ye allegn before metiond they have of their owne heads built a gallery which they say holds 104 persons. & we can find Roome but for 74 persons upon Equall compn: with ye other pews."

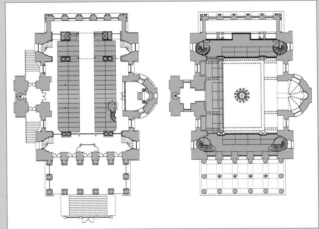

Newton, 1762

William Newton formulated a scheme which extended the north gallery to the rear, building over the vestry room. The Select Vestry, in their minutes, described:

> "for several years last past being greatly increasing in the number of its inhabitants and that the Parish Church will not now conveniently contain the Parishioners and Inhabitants there of who usually attend to hear divine service there."

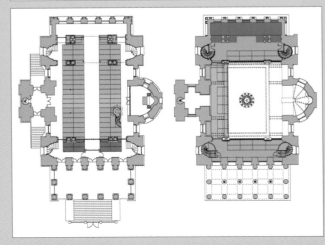

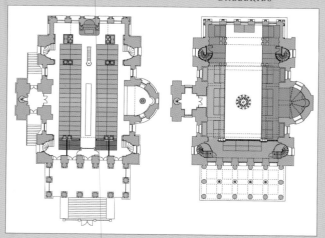

Rogers, 1776 (planned), 1782–83 (realised)

Thomas Rogers was commissioned by the Select Vestry to produce a new arrangement of the interior to accommodate even more parishioners. To facilitate this, the pews to the north of the central access had their seats and desk boards reversed. Rogers's plan described in the Faculty papers was to:

> "Take away the pews in the middle Aile under the present north gallery in order to clear obstructions from the intended situation of the altar piece pulpit Readers and Clerks Desks and to take down and remove the present Altar piece and the Appurtenances there unto belonging and fix and finish the same against the center part of the north wall."

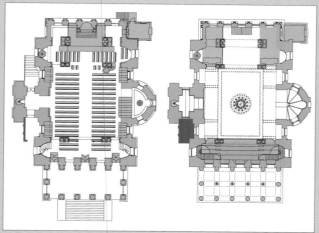

Street, 1872–75
Fitzroy-Doll, about 1886

G. E. Street's scheme removed the east, west and remaining elements of the north gallery and created a new organ loft, set lower than the old north gallery, in the north-west corner of the church. Street also raised the chancel and reredos to comply with the liturgical practice in the church. About ten years later, Charles Fitzroy-Doll was asked to further alter the gallery to improve the acoustics and rebuild the organ gallery, dividing the registers of pipes between new organ lofts in the north-west and north-east corners of the church.

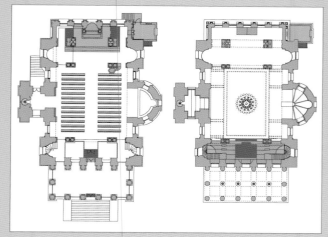

Nicholson, 1930s
King, 1952–75

By 2002 the interior of the church featured fragments of a number of rearrangements, by Charles Nicholson in the 1930s and Laurence King between 1952 and 1975. Despite many renewals of the interior, at its core survived Hawksmoor's "New Church for Bloomsbury."

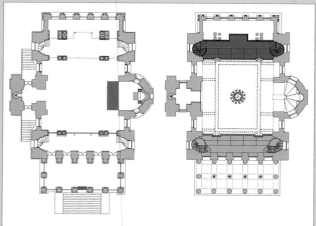

World Monuments Fund, 2002–08

With funding from the Estate of the late Paul Mellon and a range of other sources including the Heritage Lottery Fund, World Monuments Fund has conceived and led the restoration of Hawksmoor's interior, involving the reinstatement of the lost key element, the north gallery. This has recreated the intended volume and visual orientation of the principal level.

The Restoration

Gavin Stamp

The inspiration for and guiding principle in the restoration was reverence for the genius of Hawksmoor. It is always a difficult and delicate task to restore a Grade I-listed building while pleasing all the relevant authorities, historians and experts. Nevertheless, thanks to painstaking documentary research combined with detailed analysis of the surviving structure and fittings which has informed the recent restoration, it is now possible – for the first time in over two centuries – to see how brilliant was Hawksmoor's resolution of the problem of combining a traditional east-west orientation and a centralised plan with a site that was broader than it was long.

Major work was required to both the exterior and interior of St George's and repairs to the fabric and structure of the building were begun in 2002 under the direction of Colin Kerr of Molyneux Kerr, architect to St George's since 1997. Although its Portland stone walls were much weathered and coated in soot, as well as being damaged by earlier attempts at cleaning, the exterior of the church remains almost as Hawksmoor left it. Two significant losses occurred in the nineteenth century, however, which needed to be restored. The first is the south staircase to the tower, which was removed by 1811 to make way for a fire "engine house". The second restitution is symbolic rather than functional: putting back the lions and unicorns on the tower. These are heraldic beasts as they are supporters to the Royal Arms, and on the steeple they were separated by crowns on each side while they gambolled below the terminating statue of King George I, standing on his Roman altar. They could therefore be regarded as an integral part of an iconographic programme as well as an enjoyable component of the most eccentric church tower in London. As the old nursery rhyme recorded, "The Lion and the Unicorn were fighting for the crown; the Lion beat the Unicorn all around the town..."

The animated beasts carved by Edward Strong were satirised by William Hogarth in his print of *Gin Lane*, and depicted in late eighteenth-century and early nineteenth-century prints and paintings of the church, such as those by

The exterior stonework of the church was badly in need of repairs and cleaning, as seen in these views taken before work began.

TOP LEFT Detail of the northeast corner where vegetation had taken root.

TOP RIGHT The tower and the southeast corner of the portico viewed from the south.

LEFT The upper levels of the north front.

LEFT AND BELOW Views of the north front of St George's, before and during restoration.

OPPOSITE The north front after restoration, showing cleaned and repaired stonework and the newly reinstalled clear Crown glass windows.

Thomas Malton and J. M. W. Turner. Even so, although it is known that these sculptures were ten feet six inches high and that the unicorns had copper horns, no accurate detailed representations of them survive and no photographs of the exterior of St George's taken before Street's restoration have been discovered. The bold decision was therefore taken of asking a modern sculptor, Tim Crawley, to carve new lions and unicorns based on the available evidence. Carved in pieces in the artist's studio at Anglesey Abbey, these vigorous new creations have now been hoisted up and keyed in to the stonework of the stepped pyramidal Halicarnassus steeple, with triumphant success.

Recreating the original interior of Hawksmoor's church was more problematic. Although Colin Kerr considered the possibility of restoring the original orientation as well as moving the reredos back to its original location in the eastern apse, it was at first planned to have a new freestanding altar to the north, thus maintaining the reorientation of 1781. The World Monuments Fund, however, were persuaded that this was the opportunity to restore the east-west orientation of the church, and English Heritage, the Georgian Group and the parish agreed. This was also practical in so far as the original arrangement would provide more than enough space for modern congregational needs. The problem was to recover the precise appearance of the long-destroyed north gallery and other details in the absence of any original drawings or views of the interior before 1781 – a task rendered more difficult by the fact that the surviving south gallery had been altered.

The first task was to investigate the surviving documents which might provide evidence of the original interior arrangements. This comprehensive research, begun by Neil Burton of the Architectural History Practice but mostly carried out by Kevin Rogers for the World Monuments Fund, had not been done before, partly because the relevant documents are scattered. The building accounts of the 1711 Commissioners are at Lambeth Palace, but the minutes of the St George's Vestry, which record subsequent changes to the fabric, are held at Holborn Local History Library, while documents connected with the Faculties granted by the church authorities for alterations are retained at the Guildhall Library. Although none of these sources individually provides a comprehensive account of the church's building history, when read together a full, detailed picture of the changes could be established.

Similar problems were presented by the visual evidence. The surviving drawings by Hawksmoor largely depict early or preliminary designs for the building (his frequent changes of mind as the work proceeded are evident in the fabric of the building itself), but presentation drawings of the south and west elevations are in the Guildhall Library. Particularly valuable evidence was provided by the survey drawings – a carefully dimensioned plan and section – made by Thomas Rogers in 1776, prior to his reorientation, which are now in the City of Westminster Archives Centre. There are also sketches by an earlier surveyor, William Newton, who altered the seating in 1762, which are in the Drawings Collection of the Royal Institute of British Architects; these were identified as depicting the north gallery and screen to the vestry beyond, as well as the treatment of the apse. Later drawings by James Donaldson, who made a survey in 1817, and those by George Edmund Street in 1871 also survive. The

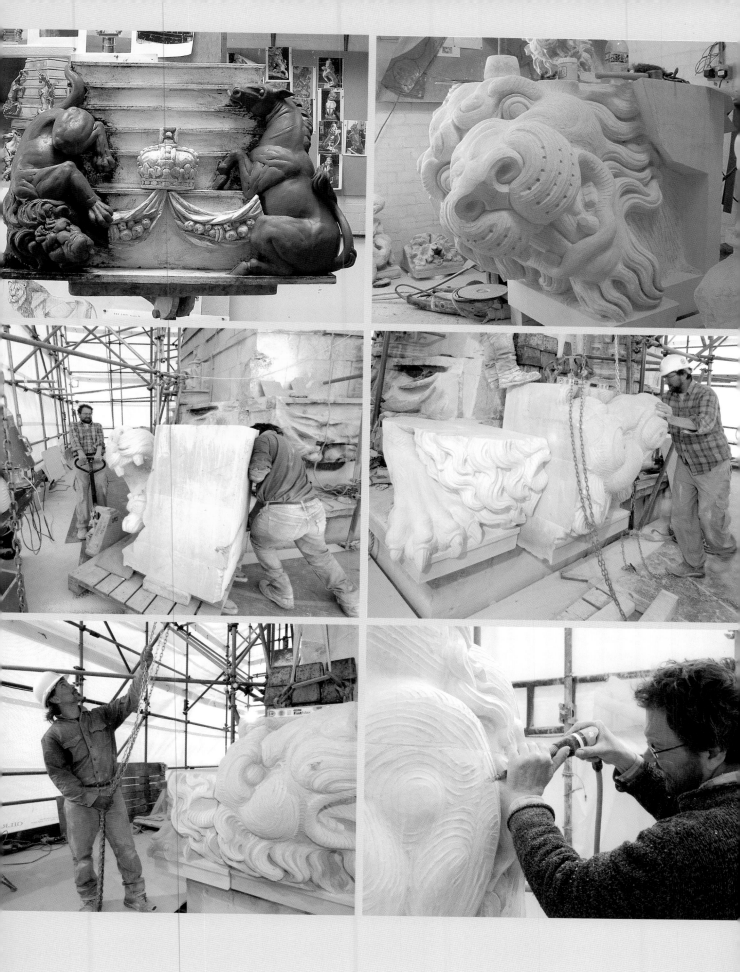

ABOVE AND RIGHT Views
of the steeple taken from the
scaffolding in May 2006, with
the installation of the lions and
unicorns complete.

ABOVE Cleaned, repaired and stripped of gilding, the reredos restored to its original position in the eastern apse. Isaac Mansfield's plasterwork can been seen in the apse above.

BELOW Detail of the reredos.

initial evidence was presented and interpreted in a Conservation Management Plan written by Stephen Gee and Peter Inskip of Inskip & Jenkins Architects. This document, which was required by the Heritage Lottery Fund and which provided a full history of the changes to the interior and presented some evidence of the original arrangement, was accepted by the parish in 2003.

The focus of the re-reoriented interior is the magnificent reredos or "altarpiece", now replaced in its original location in the eastern apse which, fortunately, retains its original elaborate decorative plasterwork by Isaac Mansfield. This reredos is more splendid and expensive than those in any other of the 1711 churches and was for long mistakenly thought to have come from the chapel in Bedford House nearby. An early example of the use of mahogany in England, combined with wainscot (or imported oak), this tall aedicular Corinthian structure contains a niche with a veneered marquetry finish. Thomas Phillips, the joiner, charged the considerable sum of £300 for it, and carving by John How cost a further £112. Repaired, cleaned, and denuded of its later gilding, the reredos has now been reunited with the flanking curved panelling in the apse, raised up on a single step. Evidence for the original arrangement is provided by Newton's survey sketch and Rogers's survey plan. The three vases which once stood on top of the pediment are long lost and, regrettably, are not to be replaced.

In front of the reredos (originally raised on two steps) once stood a timber altar table with elaborate carving, again made by Phillips and How. Regrettably, at the time of Street's 1871 reordering, this was dismantled and the carved woodwork made into two small prayer desks while the cabriole legs and the mahogany top were discarded and are now lost. It is, however, possible to reconstruct the original altar table using what remains of the original material on the basis of a drawing of it published in *The Builder* in 1888, and this is now proposed. Unfortunately, no accurate visual record survives of the long lost original altar rails with "Scroll work" for which Thomas Goff-Smith was paid £33. Modified by Street, these rails seem to have disappeared from the church in the early twentieth century.

The pulpit could not be restored to its original condition or position. Originally, it was a three-decker pulpit and stood on the south side of the nave, in front of the apse. It was raised up fourteen steps – to gallery height – on an elaborately carved hexagonal stem while, above, supported on Corinthian piers, rose a hexagonal sounding board surmounted by a vase standing on an ogee roof. Phillips was paid £140 for making this most elaborate structure, again of wainscot and mahogany, and carving cost a further £36. In the event, the base of the pulpit proved inadequate for the task and had to be strengthened; even so, when the preacher ascended the steps the thing swayed "like an enormous tulip." In the course of several subsequent moves around the church, the pulpit was cut down and placed on a stone pier. The surviving body of the pulpit has now been cleaned and repaired, but it has not been replaced in its original location as this would not conform to modern liturgical usage and would impede the flexible use of the building intended after the restoration. Nor, unfortunately, has it been possible to put back the tester or sounding board above the pulpit as this has now been lost.

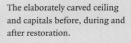

The elaborately carved ceiling and capitals before, during and after restoration.

Interiors after restoration, 2005.

LEFT The west wall, the whole composition like a giant Venetian arch.

BELOW Looking up to the top of the east wall, with the apse below.

OPPOSITE Magnificent Corinthian columns and ceiling after restoration.

LEFT View looking northeast before restoration, showing the colonnades dividing the nave from the two north aisles, with the pulpit at right.

ABOVE Wider view looking northeast, with work in progress.

BELOW LEFT AND BELOW RIGHT Laying the new floor.

OPPOSITE View looking northeast, taken in May 2008 after restoration, with the new north gallery installed between the colonnades.

ABOVE View of the south gallery after restoration, with five doors leading in from the portico. The organ has been removed from the gallery and light now streams in through the clear glass windows.

RIGHT Detail of the south gallery. The removal of the nineteenth-century brown varnish revealed this inscription from 1781, confirming the date of construction of the east gallery (which was later taken down by Street in the 1870s).

Returning the reredos to its original position made the reinstatement of the long-lost north gallery essential to recreate the original centralised square volume of Hawksmoor's nave. If this were not done, the re-established liturgical east-west axis, focussed on the altar, would be undermined by the later, and now redundant, north-south axis which would lead only to the north wall. The problem was to recover the precise design of the gallery. Careful reading of the Vestry minutes and of the Faculty documents made it certain that Thomas Rogers's 1776 drawings indicated its position and also the position of the supporting timber piers with Corinthian "grotesque capitals" carved by John How. It was also clear that Hawksmoor's north gallery was, probably, the mirror image of, and in the equivalent position to, the original south gallery as both were symmetrical about the east-west axis. Although the south gallery had been altered, first when additional galleries were added and several times subsequently, it was found that its original design could be recovered, while the supporting piers survived with their elaborate woodwork over a core of iron cast by the smith John Cleave (a remarkably early use of structural iron). Furthermore, the surviving decorative plaster ceiling underneath – the work of Isaac Mansfield – together with the survey plan indicated the position of the original timber screen which divided the nave from the five-bay lobby, or narthex, behind the portico (originally accessed by five doors, four of which were later blocked). The south gallery was also disfigured by the Victorian organ imported from another church in 1952: this has now been removed, allowing more light to enter the church from under the portico as Hawksmoor intended.

It was therefore possible to establish the appearance and design of the north gallery with a degree of certainty, assisted by reference to the building accounts and by analysis of paint samples. It emerged that the gallery fronts receded and curved behind the pairs of columns – a feature typical of Hawksmoor in that a collision between gallery and column was avoided, so maintaining the visual primacy of the structural Corinthian order. It was also evident that the curved bays at either end of the north aisle originally contained circular staircases – mirroring those in the identical bays at either end of the south aisle which allow access to the south gallery (confirmed by Inigo Meard's account for "Work done... in the four Circular Staircases to the Galleries"). However, the position of the treads was altered slightly so that more pews could be accommodated in the north gallery. Clearly the need for more seating capacity was a problem from the beginning at St George's.

Newly built spiral staircase leading up to the new north gallery.

What was more difficult to establish was the relationship between the back of the north gallery and the original vestry beyond in the extra north aisle. Newton's sketches, together with Rogers's survey, made it clear, however, that a solid Doric timber screen under the gallery with a central projection to the north separated the body of the church from the vestry beyond; this, however, has not been re-created. In the gallery itself, the panelling at the back of the pews overlooked the vestry space beyond. Above the gallery, there was no division between the north aisle and the vestry aisle below the large depressed arch: this meant that daylight from the upper tier of windows of the north wall could enter the interior.

RIGHT The rear of the north gallery, viewed from the additional aisle to the north of the nave, which originally served as the vestry aisle.

BELOW Detail of the carved Corinthian capitals on the new north gallery.

Restoring the Galleries of St George's, Bloomsbury

Peter Inskip + Peter Jenkins Architects

Background to the Reconstruction of the North Gallery

Extensive archival research and analysis of the building fabric was carried out to understand the detailing and reinstatement of Hawksmoor's north gallery. Hawksmoor's Book of Works was compared with the original bills as submitted by various craftsmen and analysed through a visual comparison of the original building fabric. The visual analysis of the original material was confirmed using paint microscopy. An understanding of the form of the gallery was gained by documenting its alteration and later removal through the survey drawings by William Newton (1762) and Thomas Rogers (1776), read in conjunction with the accounts for the alteration, the vestry minutes and the faculties for the eighteenth and nineteenth centuries. In addition, archaeology by means of paint stripping was employed to find the imprints of gallery cornices and beams left on the stone columns.

Initial design proposals made in the light of this information demonstrated the value of the original orientation and the importance of the north gallery in restoring Hawksmoor's dynamic spatial qualities, particularly the nave and double-height north bay. Such a realisation was also supported by the restoration of the plain glazing in the north and south elevation windows, helping to recover the quality of the natural light which dominated Hawksmoor's design.

Paint research on the existing south gallery identified what survived from the original construction and how much was altered, particularly by Street in 1871. The information provided with respect to the staircases showed how they directly resulted in the arrangement of the ceiling.

Structure of the South Gallery

The original eighteenth-century construction comprises iron columns supporting timber beams with their ends bearing in the flanking stone walls and stone columns within the nave. The location of the gallery structure and its supporting columns are determined by the existing alignments and the arrangements with the giant Corinthian columns of the nave to the south gallery. All of this marries with the measured drawings by Newton and Rogers. Hawksmoor particularly favoured the unusual *Grotesque* Corinthian order, executed in oak for the capital columns and cladding the iron support. Other examples of this type survive at St Mary, Woolnoth, St Alfege and St George's-in-the-East. In 1871 Street extended the gallery floors and ceilings into the stairwells, which led to the introduction of the supporting posts.

Entablature of the South Gallery

Paint microscopy shows that the entablature was modified by Street in 1871, but the majority of the existing material survives from the eighteenth century. Street altered the Order and the structure. The original architrave with a carved waterleaf motif survives on the beam ends facing the nave. He replaced the remainder with plain moulded sections, added oak architraves over the plaster frieze that run into the plaster cornice enrichments, and replaced the panelled soffits. The frieze is plain and original.

Street changed the proportion of the cornice by pulling forward the upper section to provide an over-scaled soffit that facilitated the corresponding realignment of the parapet for improving the gallery. The imprint of the original cornice arrangement of the south gallery was found on the stone Corinthian columns by raking light and paint stripping. It was decided to return the upper cornice to its original alignments, corresponding to the survey of Hawksmoor's entablature surviving at St Mary, Woolnoth.

Parapets

The front parapet of the north gallery was the same height as that on the south and accords with the dimensions on Rogers's section. This results in squarer panels than those on the existing south gallery. Rogers's sketch of the north parapet is more satisfactory than that of the existing south, and it appears that the south parapet was rebuilt by Street.

The height of the rear parapet of the north gallery was recorded in 1762 by Newton, whose sections also showed that the gallery was arranged in two tiers.

Stairs

The existing "geometric stairs" in the south gallery, with straight flights and winders, forming a U-shape in plan, do not fully confer with Hawksmoor's building accounts for "Four Circular Stairs", which were circular in plan with steps radiating from the centre. However, paint analysis has shown that the existing stairs are contemporary with the earliest scheme of decoration in the church.

Adopting the geometric stairs for the north gallery inevitably generates a three-bay ceiling arrangement, mirroring the original ceiling of the south gallery that was still surviving.

Decoration

All oak throughout the church (stairs, Grotesque Corinthian columns, panelling and wainscotting) was varnished from 1730. In the nineteenth century it was painted a stone colour and gilded lettering was inscribed on the south gallery frieze above the columns. It was later grained to imitate oak. Street, in 1871, applied a dark brown varnish to unify the old and new joinery. This has now been removed and the oak treated with boiled linseed oil, in line with eighteenth-century practice.

The undercroft after restoration. For over 100 years the coffins of many parishioners came to rest in the undercroft, but with raised awareness of public health after cholera epidemics in the mid-nineteenth century the practice was stopped and the accumulated coffins were bricked up in these arches. As part of the restoration the bricks were removed and the coffins were reburied in consecrated ground.

As for the vestry aisle itself, this narrow, double-height space seems originally to have been panelled at a lower level and divided into two rooms. The enriched plaster ceiling is original, but the architraves around the windows were added when the north wall assumed much greater importance as the background to the re-sited reredos. Today, the removal of the reredos to its original position and the reintroduction of the north gallery has allowed the extra north aisle to become a discrete volume again, and one of flexible utility for the parish.

To achieve visual harmony between the new north gallery and the existing south gallery, the late nineteenth-century darkening of the timber of the latter has been removed and the original treatment of varnished oak restored. And to complete the restoration of the interior as near as practicable to Hawksmoor's conception and thus to reinstate the original decorative schemes, colour and lighting also had to be considered. Above the line of wainscoting that ran right around the church, the Portland stone ashlar walls were painted a light stone colour. In 1765 the Vestry resolved that "the Stone Work of the inside of the Church be repaired or cleaned in a Mason like Manner so as to reduce such stonework to its Natural colour". Similarly, the plaster ceilings were painted with "whiting" or distemper. From such evidence it is clear that Hawksmoor aimed at an austere, monumental effect.

More problematic, and certainly more controversial, was the question of the glazing of the windows. Originally, daylight poured into the church through windows filled with clear Crown glass. The nineteenth century, however, preferred a dim religious light. One window of coloured patterned glass survives from a reglazing by Mawby of 1810 but most of the windows were filled with stained glass made by the distinguished firm of Clayton & Bell during or after Street's reordering of 1871–72. The upper windows are filled with geometrical patterned glass, but several windows are filled with pictorial stained glass illustrating Biblical events. At the same time, Street blocked several windows in the north wall to create a more solemn atmosphere in his reordered chancel. The resulting effect was quite contrary to Hawksmoor's intentions. On the other hand, the Clayton & Bell windows have an artistic as well as a sentimental value of their own, although it is surely justified to have removed some windows (putting them in store) to let in more daylight, as has been done.

The question of the retention or removal of Victorian stained glass highlights the philosophical problems involved with the restoration of historic buildings like St George's. There is a prejudice, particularly strong among modern architects, against recreating lost elements in a building in the style of the past. They argue that new work should be in a contemporary style in contrast to the old. At the same time it is held – often rightly – that subsequent alterations and interventions should be retained as they reflect the full, cumulative history of a building. These attitudes stem from the Manifesto of the Society for the Protection of Ancient Buildings (SPAB), founded by William Morris in 1877. Morris, however, was objecting to the widespread Victorian practice of "restoration" which all too often involved returning churches to an ideal, hypothetical state of stylistic purity by removing the later elements. Furthermore, the SPAB was at first exclusively concerned with mediaeval buildings, which are almost always cumulative creations, reflecting long and complex histories. Morris was not interested in Classical buildings; indeed, he actively disliked them and only reluctantly allowed the SPAB to campaign for the Wren churches in the City of London then threatened with demolition.

Such philosophies were responsible for the fact that most Wren churches badly damaged in the Second World War were not reconstructed authentically. Yet there is surely also a case for bringing back an historic building to its original state when that building is the work of but one great creative mind and when the original design can be convincingly reconstructed on the basis of visual and documentary evidence. This is certainly true with St George's. Fortunately, the code of practice for the modern restorer, the Burra Charter, published by Australia ICOMOS and adopted for St George's, recognises the problem. Emphasising "cultural significance", the Charter states that "*Reconstruction* is appropriate only where a *place* is incomplete through damage or alteration, and only where there is sufficient evidence to reproduce an earlier state of the *fabric*." And, thanks to the painstaking documentary research carried out, sufficient evidence has been found to restore the church interior to the way it looked in 1731, a year after its consecration.

The restoration of St George's, Bloomsbury, carried out by Molyneux Kerr together with Inskip & Jenkins Architects under the aegis of the World Monuments Fund, is deeply impressive. The monumental exterior of Portland stone has been rescued from forlorn decay and the once legendary (or notorious) heraldic beasts put back on the extraordinary steeple, while – thanks to the courageous decision to move the altar back to its original position – Hawksmoor's unusual and clever plan of the interior can now again be experienced and understood. The treatment of any historic building must be, to some degree, a subjective matter, and it has not been possible to recreate every detail of the 1731 interior. No attempt has been made to put back the long-lost box pews, for instance, as they would be inimical both to the flexibility required of the restored interior and to modern practices of worship: St George's ought not to be, and is not, a museum. The essence of Hawksmoor's original church has been revived, however, so that it is now possible again to understand, use and enjoy this most complex and subtle creation by one of England's very greatest architects.

Stonemasons, carpenters and roofers at work during the World Monument Fund's restoration of St George's.

BELOW The north front,
photographed in June 2006.

OPPOSITE View of St George's
from the south, photographed
in June 2006 as restoration was
completed. Scaffolding had just
been removed from the tower
and portico after the installation
of the lions and unicorns and
the conclusion of stone repairs
and cleaning; the last poles
and hoardings are soon to
be removed. The clean white
Portland stone gleams in the
summer sunshine.

Afterword: The Church Today and its Role in the Community

Revd Perry Butler
Rector, St George's, Bloomsbury

View of the reredos in the eastern apse, after restoration, the nave returned to its original east-west alignment.

Not so long after I came to St George's, a young Japanese student joined the congregation and was subsequently baptized and confirmed. I once asked her what had drawn her to this particular church? "Oh," she said, "when I walked by it looked so sad, and as I was feeling sad it seemed the church for me."

Certainly St George's had looked sad, forlorn and dilapidated for a good while. Over the years the external stonework had suffered erosion and damage, while the portico and the other elevations were caked black with pollution and grime. The interior seemed gloomy, its decoration tired and dated, with cracks and damp visible at high level. The lighting and heating systems were archaic and inadequate for their purpose. All in all, the glory had departed. Moreover, the immediate area seemed in the doldrums, an "inner city" area set between the West End and the City with an increasingly evident drugs problem.

The congregation was loyal but small. They had been almost three years without a resident priest when I arrived in late November 1995 as the diocese had been considering possible amalgamations. The organist had left and the caretaker was off sick (and subsequently died). Even with a new priest it was difficult in those early years to convince people that the church was open and active. I even had a telephone call from a canny property developer asking whether the building was for sale.

This was of course a marked contrast to St George's even a hundred years before. Then, the church was at the centre of the local community with a powerful social and pastoral outreach. Between the wars it tended to attract a more eclectic congregation drawn by the remarkable ministry of Father William Roberts who combined a surprisingly "open" Anglo-Catholic churchmanship (he was an early supporter of the ordination of women) with a commitment to pacifism and Christian socialism.

After the Second World War, however, congregations fell, the area changed and his successor struggled. New life came with the decision to

make the university chaplain the Rector and St George's the University church. For over a decade until the late 1960s St George's provided a lively focus for students. Many still retain fond memories of that period.

When the university left, the church reverted to its parochial role but congregations were small. Nonetheless, under Father Cooper some repair work was done including internal redecoration, repairs to the roof and some cleaning of the portico. For a tantalisingly brief period the parish experimented with an altar in the eastern apse, though it did not gain whole-hearted support. Like Father Cooper, his successor Father Chitty combined St George's with other responsibilities, and when he left the possibility of the church being made redundant was considered. However, with strong support from the then Bishop of Edmonton, the chaplain to the art colleges was appointed Priest-in-Charge and endeavoured to make St George's a centre for the visual arts, creating a gallery in the undercroft. In the twentieth century, therefore, St George's enjoyed several personas, though since the University chaplaincy period it has been far from clear what its precise role should be or how it could best serve the locality in which it is set. Despite the renewed interest in Hawksmoor it was easy to forget St George's, and the scale of the restoration that was needed seemed so daunting.

Now, in this new millennium, the church has been given the rare opportunity to rethink its entire ministry and mission. In the late 1990s the best the congregation could hope for was to raise sufficient money for emergency repairs. Our adoption by the World Monuments Fund and subsequent appearance in the 2000 Watch List was a transforming moment, though even then we had little idea what the future would hold or how exciting it would be. The generosity of the Mellon Trustees in 2001, together with the contribution of the Robert Wilson Challenge fund, the unparalleled grant from the Heritage Lottery Fund and a host of smaller donations were beyond anything we had imagined. It could easily have overwhelmed us, but with architectural and other help we were able to "think big".

The "new" St George's is now poised to regain its place as arguably the most fascinating of Hawksmoor's churches and surely one of the great churches of London. Its restoration is not only a remarkable event in itself with huge implications for the church's future religious, cultural and community life, but can only assist in the renewal of the area. St George's will take its place again as a major landmark at the heart of Bloomsbury's historic seven acres. In the future, St George's will be able to provide a richer religious ministry through word, sacrament and fellowship, and also offer much to the local residential and business communities, visitors and tourists. The Hawksmoor and Bloomsbury Exhibition, the programme of musical, cultural and educational events, and the strategic use of its ancillary spaces for different activities will all contribute to a splendid renaissance. We should be sustainable as a parish church with a sound economic base, which will ensure that the fabric remains always in good repair and the church's ministry continues and develops.

The sadness has turned into joy. The future is now bright indeed!

We are grateful.

ABOVE HRH Prince Michael of Kent, Patron of World Monuments Fund in Britain, completes the "topping-out" ceremony on the steeple on March 22, 2006 by positioning the gilded horn on the head of one of the unicorns.

OPPOSITE Finished interior showing the realigned nave leading to the western wall, and the church itself back in use.

Nicholas Hawksmoor: A Timeline

1662	Born, probably in early 1662, at East Drayton, Nottinghamshire. Worked as a clerk for Samuel Mellish, JP and Deputy Lieutenant for Yorkshire.
c.1679	Began work as a clerk to Sir Christopher Wren, who had heard of his "early skill and genius" for architecture.
1683	Employed as Deputy Surveyor to Wren at Winchester Palace.
1689	Appointed Clerk of Works at William III's palace at Kensington.
1691–1712	Assisted Wren with work on St Paul's Cathedral.
1698–1735	Clerk of Works at Greenwich Hospital.
1699	Began work assisting Sir John Vanbrugh at Castle Howard, Yorkshire.
1702	Remodelling of the exterior of Easton Neston, Northamptonshire, the original design of which was probably created in Wren's office.
1705–16	Assistant surveyor to Vanbrugh at Blenheim Palace.
1711	One of the two surveyors appointed to carry out the Fifty New Churches Act. This appointment came to an end in 1733 on the termination of the commission.
1712	Clarendon Building, Oxford.
1712–14	St Alfege, Greenwich, London.
1714–29	Christ Church, Spitalfields, London. St George's-in-the-East, London.
1714–30	St Anne's, Limehouse, London.
1715	Appointed Clerk of Works at Whitehall, Westminster and St James
1716–27	St Mary, Woolnoth, London.
1716–31	St George's, Bloomsbury, London.
1716–35	All Souls College, Oxford: North Quadrangle, Hall, Buttery and Codrington Library.
1721	Vanbrugh made Hawksmoor his deputy as Comptroller of the Works, a position which he retained until Vanbrugh's death in 1726.
1722	Took over as architect in charge of work at Blenheim Palace, after Vanbrugh's falling out with the Duchess of Marlborough.
1723	Succeeded Wren as Surveyor to Westminster Abbey.
1729–36	Mausoleum and Temple of Venus at Castle Howard.
1734	Designed the Gothic west towers of Westminster Abbey, which were completed by his successor, John James.
1736	Died of gout on March 25 at his house in Millbank. He is buried in Shenley, Hertford.